D0970384

A CHOICE OF
CHRISTINA ROSSETTI'S
VERSE

A Choice of
CHRISTINA ROSSETTI'S
Verse

Selected
with an introduction by
ELIZABETH JENNINGS

FABER AND FABER
London

First published in 1970
by Faber and Faber Limited
24 Russell Square London WC1
Printed in Great Britain by
R. MacLehose and Company Limited
The University Press Glasgow

SBN (cloth edition) 571 09017 6
SBN (paperback) 571 09018 4

Contents

7

Introduction

Christina Rossetti is a sad poet; most of her poems speak of grief or loss. Yet she can, on occasion, be surprisingly joyous, as in her famous poem called *A Birthday*:

> 'My heart is like a singing bird
> Whose nest is in a watered shoot;
> My heart is like an apple-tree
> Whose boughs are bent with thick-set fruit. . . .'

The happiness is fitful, but it is authentic for all that.

Like many, perhaps most, women poets, Christina Rossetti seems to lean towards the dark side of life; the shadows are always near. Yet this is not to say that she is a depressing poet. In some ways, however, Christina was writing at a bad time, when the influences on the poet were often not good ones. The second half of the nineteenth century was a strange period and the Pre-Raphaelite Movement made an odd, artistic group. When we look now, closely, at the paintings which emerged from this Movement (some of them painted by the poet's brother, Dante Gabriel Rossetti), we are aware of two predominant things — firstly, of a literalness of presentation, and secondly, of a melancholy in the choice of subject-matter. The period does seem, on the whole, to have been a rather unfruitful time for the arts.

Yet Christina Rossetti *could* write almost conventionally hopeful and cheerful poems, as in *Spring*:

> 'There is no time like Spring
> When life's alive in everything,
> Before new nestlings sing,
> Before cleft swallows speed their journey back
> Along the trackless track —
> God guides their wing,
> He spreads their table that they nothing lack, —
> Before the daisy grows a common flower,
> Before the sun has power
> To scorch the world up in his noontide hour.'

9

In this poem, we can see all the strength of Christina Rossetti — in the exactness of observation ('cleft swallows'), the happiness of heart that takes joy in the multitude of natural objects.

The Pre-Raphaelite Movement was a movement both of painting and of poetry. To us, now, much of the work of, say, Burne-Jones, William Morris and even of Dante Gabriel Rossetti, seems over-rich and cloying. There is altogether too much detail; too little is left to our own imaginations.

In some miraculous way, Christina Rossetti usually escaped the worst faults of the Movement. As W. W. Robson has said of her, 'So hard is it to over-praise the beauty and purity of Christina Rossetti's writings that there must be a strong temptation to over-exalt her as a poet. For she shows these qualities of sensitiveness and intelligence, in dealing with matters of deep and intimate concern to men and women, which we expect from a poet, and which we often sadly miss in the work of her larger contemporaries.'

Here, we have, then, a poet of unusual talent who was born at a time when it was difficult to write really great poetry. Yet, for Christina Rossetti, it was not only possible to write sincere and deeply felt work, but also to build up a considerable œuvre of verse. It is hard to choose a selection from her numerous poems because so many of them are of the same fine quality. Like other women poets, such as Emily Dickinson and Charlotte Mew, she is always close to the melancholy, the withdrawn, the broken things. But she is also capable of a great delight in life — a delight which is, perhaps, accentuated by her moments of sadness — and this she shares with us abundantly.

Christina Georgina Rossetti was born on 5 December, 1830, the youngest child of Gabriele Rossetti. Her family, particularly her brothers, were to play a large part in her future life; she never really broke away from her home and all that it signified.

It is not, I think, surprising that Christina wrote some charming poems for children in the book called *Sing-Song. Goblin Market*, though it is often set before children at school is not, to my idea, a poem for young people at all; it is an adult, short epic which happens to make use of fairies and goblins. But *Sing-Song* contains some verses perfectly designed for children, such as,

> 'O wind, where have you been,
>   That you blow so sweet?
> Among the violets
>   Which blossom at your feet.'

Goblin Market is the longest poem which Christina Rossetti wrote. The poem contains many felicities, but not, in general, those which a child would appreciate. The most obvious quality of the poem is its sensuousness:

> 'You cannot think what figs
> My teeth have met in,
> What melons icy-cold
> Piled on a dish of gold
> Too huge for me to hold,
> What peaches with a velvet nap,
> Pellucid grapes without one seed. . . .'

How Keatsian all this is, and how precise; 'Peaches with a velvet nap' is a perfect description of the fruit.

Christina Rossetti's poetic output was, as I have indicated, fairly large. One is, somehow, rather surprised by this, perhaps because she has so often only appeared in anthologies. Her most famous poems are *Goblin Market* and *A Birthday*. Little else seems to be widely known, even by the most avid reader of poetry.

Christina Rossetti had two semi-amorous relations with men during her life. But she remained single, inviolate. That she knew all about the vagaries of love and passion, there is no doubt at all. But she seldom writes of reciprocated love.

Christina was more fortunate than many poets, since she lived in a home which actively encouraged the arts. As Georgina Battiscombe has pointed out, Christina was the least intellectual of the family of two girls and two boys. She and her sister, Maria, were educated by their mother and they were encouraged to follow Anglo-Catholicism. Later, in fact, Christina rejected two offers of marriage purely on religious grounds. Her life was, thus, extremely sheltered and centred on her brothers and sister.

Christina is not a very popular poet today. Her work, to many people, seems extremely dated. Yet, she is well worth exploring for the many felicities in her poems and for the perfection of her lyric ear; at her time, no other poet but Tennyson had a more flawless sense of sound. Her subjects were limited, it is true, but she never made the mistake of writing beyond the limits of her experience. She always stayed well within her scope, and it was not so limited after all, since she ranged through many worlds, many subjects. She is certainly due for a revival.

There still remain large questions to ask and, to try to answer. Why, for example, did Christina Rossetti never move away from the gentle passions (if one can so call them) of lost or unrequited love? We know, from her life, that she did have two unhappy love-affairs. They seem only to have tempted her to an even greater melancholy of temper than she was usually accustomed to. Over all her work, even the most moving, lie this sense of something lost. It may be that this is the reason why no-one has ever felt inclined to call her a really great poet; that she has been, and is greatly admired, goes without question.

Probably, we are not sufficiently grateful to our minor poets; they often show us our great ones in miniature, as it were. Christina Rossetti is certainly in the forefront of minor late nineteenth-century English poets. There can never be any dispute on this point.

Lona Mosk Packer, in her exhaustive biography of Christina Rossetti, has striven to prove that she was a great poet. I do not believe that she has succeeded. Christina has not the scope, the depth, the variety, of a truly great writer. Yet Miss Packer's book has done much to clear the ground for other critics. She also points out the importance of William Rossetti, Christina's brother, as her editor. I do not think that Miss Packer's searchings of Christina's abortive love-affairs really add to our knowledge of the poet. The poems speak for themselves.

ELIZABETH JENNINGS

Goblin Market

Morning and evening
Maids heard the goblins cry:
'Come buy our orchard fruits,
Come buy, come buy:
Apples and quinces,
Lemons and oranges,
Plump unpecked cherries,
Melons and raspberries,
Bloom-down-cheeked peaches,
Swart-headed mulberries,
Wild free-born cranberries,
Crab-apples, dewberries,
Pine-apples, blackberries,
Apricots, strawberries; —
All ripe together
In summer weather, —
Morns that pass by,
Fair eves that fly;
Come buy, come buy:
Our grapes fresh from the vine,
Pomegranates full and fine,
Dates and sharp bullaces,
Rare pears and greengages,
Damsons and bilberries,
Taste them and try:
Currants and gooseberries,
Bright-fire-like barberries,
Figs to fill your mouth,
Citrons from the South,
Sweet to tongue and sound to eye;
Come buy, come buy.'

Evening by evening
Among the brookside rushes,
Laura bowed her head to hear,

Lizzie veiled her blushes:
Crouching close together
In the cooling weather,
With clasping arms and cautioning lips,
With tingling cheeks and finger tips.
'Lie close,' Laura said,
Pricking up her golden head:
'We must not look at goblin men,
We must not buy their fruits:
Who knows upon what soil they fed
Their hungry thirsty roots?'
'Come buy,' call the goblins
Hobbling down the glen.
'Oh,' cried Lizzie, 'Laura, Laura,
You should not peep at goblin men.'
Lizzie covered up her eyes,
Covered close lest they should look;
Laura reared her glossy head,
And whispered like the restless brook:
'Look, Lizzie, look, Lizzie,
Down the glen tramp little men.
One hauls a basket,
One bears a plate,
One lugs a golden dish
Of many pounds weight.
How fair the vine must grow
Whose grapes are so luscious;
How warm the wind must blow
Through those fruit bushes.'
'No,' said Lizzie: 'No, no, no;
Their offers should not charm us,
Their evil gifts would harm us.'
She thrust a dimpled finger
In each ear, shut eyes and ran:
Curious Laura chose to linger
Wondering at each merchant man.
One had a cat's face,
One whisked a tail,

One tramped at a rat's pace,
One crawled like a snail,
One like a wombat prowled obtuse and furry,
One like a ratel tumbled hurry skurry.
She heard a voice like voice of doves
Cooing all together:
They sounded kind and full of loves
In the pleasant weather.

Laura stretched her gleaming neck
Like a rush-imbedded swan,
Like a lily from the beck,
Like a moonlit poplar branch,
Like a vessel at the launch
When its last restraint is gone.

Backwards up the mossy glen
Turned and trooped the goblin men,
With their shrill repeated cry,
'Come buy, come buy.'
When they reached where Laura was
They stood stock still upon the moss,
Leering at each other,
Brother with queer brother;
Signalling each other,
Brother with sly brother.
One set his basket down,
One reared his plate;
One began to weave a crown
Of tendrils, leaves, and rough nuts brown
(Men sell not such in any town);
One heaved the golden weight
Of dish and fruit to offer her:
'Come buy, come buy,' was still their cry.
Laura stared but did not stir,
Longed but had no money:
The whisk-tailed merchant bade her taste

In tones as smooth as honey,
The cat-faced purr'd,
The rat-paced spoke a word
Of welcome, and the snail-paced even was heard;
One parrot-voiced and jolly
Cried 'Pretty Goblin' still for 'Pretty Polly;' —
One whistled like a bird.

But sweet-tooth Laura spoke in haste:
'Good folk, I have no coin;
To take were to purloin:
I have no copper in my purse,
I have no silver either,
And all my gold is on the furze
That shakes in windy weather
Above the rusty heather.'
'You have much gold upon your head,'
They answered all together:
'Buy from us with a golden curl.'
She clipped a precious golden lock,
She dropped a tear more rare than pearl,
Then sucked their fruit globes fair or red:
Sweeter than honey from the rock,
Stronger than man-rejoicing wine,
Clearer than water flowed that juice;
She never tasted such before,
How should it cloy with length of use?
She sucked and sucked and sucked the more
Fruits which that unknown orchard bore;
She sucked until her lips were sore;
Then flung the emptied rinds away
But gathered up one kernel stone,
And knew not was it night or day
As she turned home alone.

Lizzie met her at the gate
Full of wise upbraidings:
'Dear, you should not stay so late,

Twilight is not good for maidens;
Should not loiter in the glen
In the haunts of goblin men.
Do you not remember Jeanie,
How she met them in the moonlight,
Took their gifts both choice and many,
Ate their fruits and wore their flowers
Plucked from bowers
Where summer ripens at all hours?
But ever in the noonlight
She pined and pined away;
Sought them by night and day,
Found them no more but dwindled and grew grey;
Then fell with the first snow,
While to this day no grass will grow
Where she lies low:
I planted daisies there a year ago
That never blow.
You should not loiter so.'
'Nay, hush,' said Laura:
'Nay, hush, my sister:
I ate and ate my fill,
Yet my mouth waters still;
To-morrow night I will
Buy more:' and kissed her:
'Have done with sorrow;
I'll bring you plums to-morrow
Fresh on their mother twigs,
Cherries worth getting;
You cannot think what figs
My teeth have met in,
What melons icy-cold
Piled on a dish of gold
Too huge for me to hold,
What peaches with a velvet nap,
Pellucid grapes without one seed:
Odorous indeed must be the mead
Whereon they grow, and pure the wave they drink

With lilies at the brink,
And sugar-sweet their sap.'

Golden head by golden head,
Like two pigeons in one nest
Folded in each other's wings,
They lay down in their curtained bed:
Like two blossoms on one stem,
Like two flakes of new-fall'n snow,
Like two wands of ivory
Tipped with gold for awful kings.
Moon and stars gazed in at them,
Wind sang to them lullaby,
Lumbering owls forbore to fly,
Not a bat flapped to and fro
Round their nest:
Cheek to cheek and breast to breast
Locked together in one nest.

Early in the morning
When the first cock crowed his warning,
Neat like bees, as sweet and busy,
Laura rose with Lizzie:
Fetched in honey, milked the cows,
Aired and set to rights the house,
Kneaded cakes of whitest wheat,
Cake for dainty mouths to eat,
Next churned butter, whipped up cream,
Fed their poultry, sat and sewed;
Talked as modest maidens should:
Lizzie with an open heart,
Laura in an absent dream,
One content, one sick in part;
One warbling for the mere bright day's delight,
One longing for the night.

At length slow evening came:
They went with pitchers to the reedy brook;

Lizzie most placid in her look,
Laura most like a leaping flame.
They drew the gurgling water from its deep;
Lizzie plucked purple and rich golden flags,
Then turning homewards said: 'The sunset flushes
Those furthest loftiest crags;
Come, Laura, not another maiden lags,
No wilful squirrel wags,
The beasts and birds are fast asleep.'
But Laura loitered still among the rushes
And said the bank was steep.

And said the hour was early still,
The dew not fall'n, the wind not chill:
Listening ever, but not catching
The customary cry,
'Come buy, come buy,'
With its iterated jingle
Of sugar-baited words:
Not for all her watching
Once discerning even one goblin
Racing, whisking, tumbling, hobbling;
Let alone the herds
That used to tramp along the glen,
In groups or single,
Of brisk fruit-merchant men.

Till Lizzie urged, 'O Laura, come;
I hear the fruit-call but I dare not look:
You should not loiter longer at this brook:
Come with me home.
The stars rise, the moon bends her arc,
Each glowworm winks her spark,
Let us get home before the night grows dark:
For clouds may gather
Though this is summer weather,
Put out the lights and drench us through;
Then if we lost our way what should we do?'

19

Laura turned cold as stone
To find her sister heard that cry alone,
That goblin cry,
'Come buy our fruits, come buy.'
Must she then buy no more such dainty fruit?
Must she no more such succous pasture find,
Gone deaf and blind?
Her tree of life drooped from the root:
She said not one word in her heart's sore ache;
But peering thro' the dimness, nought discerning,
Trudged home, her pitcher dripping all the way;
So crept to bed, and lay
Silent till Lizzie slept;
Then sat up in a passionate yearning,
And gnashed her teeth for baulked desire, and wept
As if her heart would break.

Day after day, night after night,
Laura kept watch in vain
In sullen silence of exceeding pain.
She never caught again the goblin cry:
'Come buy, come buy;' —
She never spied the goblin men
Hawking their fruits along the glen:
But when the noon waxed bright
Her hair grew thin and grey;
She dwindled, as the fair full moon doth turn
To swift decay and burn
Her fire away.

One day remembering her kernel-stone
She set it by a wall that faced the south;
Dewed it with tears, hoped for a root,
Watched for a waxing shoot,
But there came none;
It never saw the sun,
It never felt the trickling moisture run:
While with sunk eyes and faded mouth

She dreamed of melons, as a traveller sees
False waves in desert drouth
With shade of leaf-crowned trees,
And burns the thirstier in the sandful breeze.

She no more swept the house,
Tended the fowls or cows,
Fetched honey, kneaded cakes of wheat,
Brought water from the brook:
But sat down listless in the chimney-nook
And would not eat.

Tender Lizzie could not bear
To watch her sister's cankerous care
Yet not to share.
She night and morning
Caught the goblins' cry:
'Come buy our orchard fruits,
Come buy, come buy:' —
Beside the brook, along the glen,
She heard the tramp of goblin men,
The voice and stir
Poor Laura could not hear;
Longed to buy fruit to comfort her,
But feared to pay too dear.
She thought of Jeanie in her grave,
Who should have been a bride;
But who for joys brides hope to have
Fell sick and died
In her gay prime,
In earliest Winter time,
With the first glazing rime,
With the first snow-fall of crisp Winter time.

Till Laura dwindling
Seemed knocking at Death's door:
Then Lizzie weighed no more
Better and worse;

But put a silver penny in her purse,
Kissed Laura, crossed the heath with clumps of furze
At twilight, halted by the brook:
And for the first time in her life
Began to listen and look.

Laughed every goblin
When they spied her peeping:
Came towards her hobbling,
Flying, running, leaping,
Puffing and blowing,
Chuckling, clapping, crowing,
Clucking and gobbling,
Mopping and mowing,
Full of airs and graces,
Pulling wry faces,
Demure grimaces,
Cat-like and rat-like,
Ratel- and wombat-like,
Snail-paced in a hurry,
Parrot-voiced and whistler,
Helter skelter, hurry skurry,
Chattering like magpies,
Fluttering like pigeons,
Gliding like fishes, —
Hugged her and kissed her:
Squeezed and caressed her:
Stretched up their dishes,
Panniers, and plates:
'Look at our apples
Russet and dun,
Bob at our cherries,
Bite at our peaches,
Citrons and dates,
Grapes for the asking,
Pears red with basking
Out in the sun,
Plums on their twigs;

22

Pluck them and suck them,
Pomegranates, figs.' —

  'Good folk,' said Lizzie,
Mindful of Jeanie:
'Give me much and many:' —
Held out her apron,
Tossed them her penny.
'Nay, take a seat with us,
Honour and eat with us,'
They answered grinning:
'Our feast is but beginning.
Night yet is early,
Warm and dew-pearly,
 Wakeful and starry:
Such fruits as these
No man can carry;
Half their bloom would fly,
Half their dew would dry,
Half their flavour would pass by.
Sit down and feast with us,
Be welcome guest with us,
Cheer you and rest with us.' —
'Thank you,' said Lizzie: 'But one waits
At home alone for me:
So without further parleying,
If you will not sell me any
Of your fruits though much and many,
Give me back my silver penny
I tossed you for a fee.' —
They began to scratch their pates,
No longer wagging, purring,
But visibly demurring,
Grunting and snarling.
One called her proud,
Cross-grained, uncivil;
Their tones waxed loud,
Their looks were evil.

Lashing their tails
They trod and hustled her,
Elbowed and jostled her,
Clawed with their nails,
Barking, mewing, hissing, mocking,
Tore her gown and soiled her stocking,
Twitched her hair out by the roots,
Stamped upon her tender feet,
Held her hands and squeezed their fruits
Against her mouth to make her eat.

White and golden Lizzie stood,
Like a lily in a flood, —
Like a rock of blue-veined stone
Lashed by tides obstreperously, —
Like a beacon left alone
In a hoary roaring sea,
Sending up a golden fire, —
Like a fruit-crowned orange-tree
White with blossoms honey-sweet
Sore beset by wasp and bee, —
Like a royal virgin town
Topped with gilded dome and spire
Close beleaguered by a fleet
Mad to tug her standard down.

One may lead a horse to water,
Twenty cannot make him drink.
Though the goblins cuffed and caught her,
Coaxed and fought her,
Bullied and besought her,
Scratched her, pinched her black as ink,
Kicked and knocked her,
Mauled and mocked her,
Lizzie uttered not a word;
Would not open lip from lip
Lest they should cram a mouthful in:
But laughed in heart to feel the drip

Of juice that syrupped all her face,
And lodged in dimples of her chin,
And streaked her neck which quaked like curd.
At last the evil people
Worn out by her resistance
Flung back her penny, kicked their fruit
Along whichever road they took,
Not leaving root or stone or shoot;
Some writhed into the ground,
Some dived into the brook
With ring and ripple,
Some scudded on the gale without a sound,
Some vanished in the distance.

In a smart, ache, tingle,
Lizzie went her way;
Knew not was it night or day;
Sprang up the bank, tore thro' the furze,
Threaded copse and dingle,
And heard her penny jingle
Bouncing in her purse, —
Its bounce was music to her ear.
She ran and ran
As if she feared some goblin man
Dogged her with gibe or curse
Or something worse:
But not one goblin skurried after,
Nor was she pricked by fear;
The kind heart made her windy-paced
That urged her home quite out of breath with haste
And inward laughter.

She cried 'Laura,' up the garden,
'Did you miss me?
Come and kiss me.
Never mind my bruises,
Hug me, kiss me, suck my juices
Squeezed from goblin fruits for you,

Goblin pulp and goblin dew.
Eat me, drink me, love me;
Laura, make much of me:
For your sake I have braved the glen
And had to do with goblin merchant men.'

Laura started from her chair,
Flung her arms up in the air,
Clutched her hair:
'Lizzie, Lizzie, have you tasted
For my sake the fruit forbidden?
Must your light like mine be hidden,
Your young life like mine be wasted,
Undone in mine undoing
And ruined in my ruin,
Thirsty, cankered, goblin-ridden?' —
She clung about her sister,
Kissed and kissed and kissed her:
Tears once again
Refreshed her shrunken eyes,
Dropping like rain
After long sultry drouth;
Shaking with anguish fear, and pain,
She kissed and kissed her with a hungry mouth.

Her lips began to scorch,
That juice was wormwood to her tongue,
She loathed the feast:
Writhing as one possessed she leaped and sung,
Rent all her robe, and wrung
Her hands in lamentable haste,
And beat her breast.
Her locks streamed like the torch
Borne by a racer at full speed,
Or like the mane of horses in their flight,
Or like an eagle when she stems the light
Straight toward the sun,

Or like a caged thing freed,
Or like a flying flag when armies run.

   Swift fire spread through her veins, knocked at
      her heart,
Met the fire smouldering there
And overbore its lesser flame;
She gorged on bitterness without a name:
Ah! fool, to choose such part
Of soul-consuming care!
Sense failed in the mortal strife:
Like the watch-tower of a town
Which an earthquake shatters down,
Like a lightning-stricken mast,
Like a wind-uprooted tree
Spun about,
Like a foam-topped waterspout
Cast down headlong in the sea,
She fell at last;
Pleasure past and anguish past,
Is it death or is it life?

   Life out of death.
That night long Lizzie watched by her,
Counted her pulse's flagging stir,
Felt for her breath,
Held water to her lips, and cooled her face
With tears and fanning leaves:
But when the first birds chirped about their eaves,
And early reapers plodded to the place
Of golden sheaves,
And dew-wet grass
Bowed in the morning winds so brisk to pass,
And new buds with new day
Opened of cup-like lilies on the stream,
Laura awoke as from a dream,
Laughed in the innocent old way,
Hugged Lizzie but not twice or thrice;

Her gleaming locks showed not one thread of grey,
Her breath was sweet as May
And light danced in her eyes.

   Days, weeks, months, years
Afterwards, when both were wives
With children of their own;
Their mother-hearts beset with fears,
Their lives bound up in tender lives;
Laura would call the little ones
And tell them of her early prime,
Those pleasant days long gone
Of not-returning time:
Would talk about the haunted glen,
The wicked, quaint fruit-merchant men,
Their fruits like honey to the throat
But poison in the blood;
(Men sell not such in any town:)
Would tell them how her sister stood
In deadly peril to do her good,
And win the fiery antidote:
Then joining hands to little hands
Would bid them cling together,
'For there is no friend like a sister
In calm or stormy weather;
To cheer one on the tedious way,
To fetch one if one goes astray,
To lift one if one totters down,
To strengthen whilst one stands.'

Dream Land

Where sunless rivers weep
Their waves into the deep,
She sleeps a charmèd sleep:
   Awake her not.
Led by a single star,
She came from very far
To seek where shadows are
   Her pleasant lot.

She left the rosy morn,
She left the fields of corn,
For twilight cold and lorn
   And water springs.
Through sleep, as through a veil,
She sees the sky look pale,
And hears the nightingale
   That sadly sings.

Rest, rest, a perfect rest
Shed over brow and breast;
Her face is toward the west,
   The purple land.
She cannot see the grain
Ripening on hill and plain;
She cannot feel the rain
   Upon her hand.

Rest, rest, for evermore
Upon a mossy shore;
Rest, rest at the heart's core
   Till time shall cease:
Sleep that no pain shall wake,
Night that no morn shall break
Till joy shall overtake
   Her perfect peace.

At Home

When I was dead, my spirit turned
  To seek the much-frequented house:
I passed the door, and saw my friends
  Feasting beneath the green orange boughs;
From hand to hand they pushed the wine,
  They sucked the pulp of plum and peach;
They sang, they jested, and they laughed,
  For each was loved of each.

I listened to their honest chat:
  Said one: 'To-morrow we shall be
Plod plod along the featureless sands
  And coasting miles and miles of sea.'
Said one: 'Before the turn of tide
  We will achieve the eyrie-seat.'
Said one: 'To-morrow shall be like
  To-day, but much more sweet.'

'To-morrow,' said they, strong with hope,
  And dwelt upon the pleasant way:
'To-morrow,' cried they one and all,
  While no one spoke of yesterday.
Their life stood full at blessed noon;
  I, only I, had passed away:
'To-morrow and to-day,' they cried;
  I was of yesterday.

I shivered comfortless, but cast
  No chill across the tablecloth;
I all-forgotten shivered, sad
  To stay and yet to part how loth:
I passed from the familiar room,
I who from love had passed away,

Like the remembrance of a guest
   That tarrieth but a day.

A Triad

SONNET

Three sang of love together: one with lips
   Crimson, with cheeks and bosom in a glow,
Flushed to the yellow hair and finger-tips;
   And one there sang who soft and smooth as snow
   Bloomed like a tinted hyacinth at a show;
And one was blue with famine after love,
   Who like a harpstring snapped rang harsh and low
The burden of what those were singing of.
One shamed herself in love; one temperately
   Grew gross in soulless love, a sluggish wife;
One famished died for love. Thus two of three
   Took death for love and won him after strife;
One droned in sweetness like a fattened bee:
   All on the threshold, yet all short of life.

Cousin Kate

I was a cottage maiden
   Hardened by sun and air,
Contented with my cottage mates,
   Not mindful I was fair.
Why did a great lord find me out,
   And praise my flaxen hair?
Why did a great lord find me out
   To fill my heart with care?

31

He lured me to his palace home —
  Woe's me for joy thereof —
To lead a shameless shameful life,
  His plaything and his love.
He wore me like a silken knot,
  He changed me like a glove;
So now I moan, an unclean thing,
  Who might have been a dove.

O Lady Kate, my cousin Kate,
  You grew more fair than I:
He saw you at your father's gate,
  Chose you, and cast me by.
He watched your steps along the lane,
  Your work among the rye;
He lifted you from mean estate
  To sit with him on high.

Because you were so good and pure
  He bound you with his ring:
The neighbours call you good and pure,
  Call me an outcast thing.
Even so I sit and howl in dust,
  You sit in gold and sing:
Now which of us has tenderer heart?
  You had the stronger wing.

O cousin Kate, my love was true,
  Your love was writ in sand:
If he had fooled not me but you,
  If you stood where I stand,
He'd not have won me with his love
  Nor bought me with his land;
I would have spit into his face
  And not have taken his hand.

Yet I've a gift you have not got,
  And seem not like to get:
For all your clothes and wedding-ring
  I've little doubt you fret.
My fair-haired son, my shame, my pride,
  Cling closer, closer yet:
Your father would give lands for one
  To wear his coronet.

Noble Sisters

'Now did you mark a falcon,
  Sister dear, sister dear,
Flying toward my window
  In the morning cool and clear?
With jingling bells about her neck,
  But what beneath her wing?
It may have been a ribbon,
  Or it may have been a ring.' —
    'I marked a falcon swooping
      At the break of day:
    And for your love, my sister dove,
      I 'frayed the thief away.' —

'Or did you spy a ruddy hound,
  Sister fair and tall,
Went snuffing round my garden bound,
  Or crouched by my bower wall?
With a silken leash about his neck;
  But in his mouth may be
A chain of gold and silver links,
  Or a letter writ to me.' —
    'I heard a hound, highborn sister,
      Stood baying at the moon:
    I rose and drove him from your wall
      Lest you should wake too soon.' —

'Or did you meet a pretty page
    Sat swinging on the gate;
Sat whistling whistling like a bird,
    Or may be slept too late:
With eaglets broidered on his cap,
    And eaglets on his glove?
If you had turned his pockets out,
    You had found some pledge of love.' —
        'I met him at this daybreak,
            Scarce the east was red:
            Lest the creaking gate should anger you,
            I packed him home to bed.' —

'Oh patience sister. Did you see
    A young man tall and strong,
Swift-footed to uphold the right
    And to uproot the wrong,
Come home across the desolate sea
    To woo me for his wife?
And in his heart my heart is locked,
    And in his life my life.' —
        'I met a nameless man, sister,
            Hard by your chamber door:
            I said: Her husband loves her much.
            And yet she loves him more.' —

'Fie, sister, fie, a wicked lie,
    A lie, a wicked lie,
I have none other love but him,
    Nor will have till I die.
And you have turned him from our door,
    And stabbed him with a lie:
I will go seek him thro' the world
    In sorrow till I die.' —
        'Go seek in sorrow, sister,
            And find in sorrow too:
            If thus you shame our father's name
            My curse go forth with you.'

Spring

Frost-locked all the winter,
Seeds, and roots, and stones of fruits,
What shall make their sap ascend
That they may put forth shoots?
Tips of tender green,
Leaf, or blade, or sheath;
Telling of the hidden life
That breaks forth underneath,
Life nursed in its grave by Death.

Blows the thaw-wind pleasantly,
Drips the soaking rain,
By fits looks down the waking sun:
Young grass springs on the plain;
Young leaves clothe early hedgerow trees;
Seeds, and roots, and stones of fruits,
Swollen with sap put forth their shoots;
Curled-headed ferns sprout in the lane;
Birds sing and pair again.

There is no time like Spring,
When life's alive in everything,
Before new nestlings sing,
Before cleft swallows speed their journey back
Along the trackless track —
God guides their wing,
He spreads their table that they nothing lack, —
Before the daisy grows a common flower,
Before the sun has power
To scorch the world up in his noontide hour.

There is no time like Spring,
Like Spring that passes by:
There is no life like Spring-life born to die, —
Piercing the sod,

Clothing the uncouth clod,
Hatched in the nest,
Fledged on the windy bough,
Strong on the wing;
There is no time like Spring that passes by,
Now newly born, and now
Hastening to die.

A Birthday

My heart is like a singing bird
   Whose nest is in a watered shoot;
My heart is like an apple-tree
   Whose boughs are bent with thick-set fruit;
My heart is like a rainbow shell
   That paddles in a halcyon sea;
My heart is gladder than all these
   Because my love is come to me.

Raise me a dais of silk and down;
   Hang it with vair and purple dyes;
Carve it in doves, and pomegranates,
   And peacocks with a hundred eyes;
Work it in gold and silver grapes,
   In leaves, and silver fleurs-de-lys;
Because the birthday of my life
   Is come, my love is come to me.

Remember

Remember me when I am gone away,
  Gone far away into the silent land;
  When you can no more hold me by the hand,
Nor I half turn to go yet turning stay.
Remember me when no more day by day
  You tell me of our future that you planned:
  Only remember me; you understand
It will be late to counsel then or pray.
Yet if you should forget me for a while
  And afterwards remember, do not grieve:
  For if the darkness and corruption leave
  A vestige of the thoughts that once I had,
Better by far you should forget and smile
  Than that you should remember and be sad.

After Death

SONNET

The curtains were half drawn, the floor was swept
  And strewn with rushes, rosemary and may
  Lay thick upon the bed on which I lay,
Where through the lattice ivy-shadows crept.
He leaned above me, thinking that I slept
  And could not hear him; but I heard him say:
  'Poor child, poor child:' and as he turned away
Came a deep silence, and I knew he wept.
He did not touch the shroud, or raise the fold
  That hid my face, or take my hand in his,
    Or ruffle the smooth pillows for my head:
    He did not love me living; but once dead
  He pitied me; and very sweet it is
To know he still is warm though I am cold.

An End

Love, strong as Death, is dead.
Come, let us make his bed
Among the dying flowers:
A green turf at his head;
And a stone at his feet,
Whereon we may sit
In the quiet evening hours.

He was born in the Spring,
And died before the harvesting:
On the last warm summer day
He left us; he would not stay
For Autumn twilight cold and grey.
Sit we by his grave, and sing
He is gone away.

To few chords and sad and low
Sing we so:
Be our eyes fixed on the grass
Shadow-veiled as the years pass
While we think of all that was
In the long ago.

My Dream

Hear now a curious dream I dreamed last night
Each word whereof is weighed and sifted truth.

I stood beside Euphrates while it swelled
Like overflowing Jordan in its youth:
It waxed and coloured sensibly to sight;
Till out of myriad pregnant waves there welled

Young crocodiles, a gaunt blunt-featured crew,
Fresh-hatched perhaps and daubed with birthday dew.
The rest if I should tell, I fear my friend
My closest friend would deem the facts untrue;
And therefore it were wisely left untold;
Yet if you will, why, hear it to the end.

  Each crocodile was girt with massive gold
And polished stones that with their wearers grew:
But one there was who waxed beyond the rest,
Wore kinglier girdle and a kingly crown,
Whilst crowns and orbs and sceptres starred his breast.
All gleamed compact and green with scale on scale,
But special burnishment adorned his mail
And special terror weighed upon his frown;
His punier brethren quaked before his tail,
Broad as a rafter, potent as a flail.
So he grew lord and master of his kin:
But who shall tell the tale of all their woes?
An execrable appetite arose,
He battened on them, crunched, and sucked them in.
He knew no law, he feared no binding law,
But ground them with inexorable jaw:
The luscious fat distilled upon his chin,
Exuded from his nostrils and his eyes,
While still like hungry death he fed his maw;
Till every minor crocodile being dead
And buried too, himself gorged to the full,
He slept with breath oppressed and unstrung claw.
Oh marvel passing strange which next I saw:
In sleep he dwindled to the common size,
And all the empire faded from his coat.
Then from far off a wingèd vessel came,
Swift as a swallow subtle as a flame:
I know not what it bore of freight or host,
But white it was as an avenging ghost.
It levelled strong Euphrates in its course;
Supreme yet weightless as an idle mote

It seemed to tame the waters without force
Till not a murmur swelled or billow beat:
Lo, as the purple shadow swept the sands,
The prudent crocodile rose on his feet
And shed appropriate tears and wrung his hands.

What can it mean? you ask. I answer not
For meaning, but myself must echo, What?
And tell it as I saw it on the spot.

Song

Oh roses for the flush of youth,
    And laurel for the perfect prime;
But pluck an ivy branch for me
    Grown old before my time.

Oh violets for the grave of youth,
    And bay for those dead in their prime;
Give me the withered leaves I chose
    Before in the old time.

A Summer Wish

Live all thy sweet life thro',
    Sweet Rose, dew-sprent,
Drop down thine evening dew
To gather it anew
When day is bright:
    I fancy thou wast meant
Chiefly to give delight.

Sing in the silent sky,
  Glad soaring bird;
Sing out thy notes on high
To sunbeam straying by
Or passing cloud;
  Heedless if thou art heard
Sing thy full song aloud.

Oh that it were with me
  As with the flower;
Blooming on its own tree
For butterfly and bee
Its summer morns:
  That I might bloom mine hour
A rose in spite of thorns.

Oh that my work were done
  As birds' that soar
Rejoicing in the sun:
That when my time is run
And daylight too,
  I so might rest once more
Cool with refreshing dew.

An Apple Gathering

I plucked pink blossoms from mine apple-tree
  And wore them all that evening in my hair:
Then in due season when I went to see
  I found no apples there.

With dangling basket all along the grass
  As I had come I went the selfsame track:
My neighbours mocked me while they saw me pass
  So empty-handed back.

Lilian and Lilias smiled in trudging by,
    Their heaped-up basket teased me like a jeer;
Sweet-voiced they sang beneath the sunset sky,
    Their mother's home was near.

Plump Gertrude passed me with her basket full,
    A stronger hand than hers helped it along;
A voice talked with her through the shadows cool
    More sweet to me than song.

Ah Willie, Willie, was my love less worth
    Than apples with their green leaves piled above?
I counted rosiest apples on the earth
    Of far less worth than love.

So once it was with me you stooped to talk
    Laughing and listening in this very lane:
To think that by this way we used to walk
    We shall not walk again!

I let my neighbours pass me, ones and twos
    And groups; the latest said the night grew chill,
And hastened: but I loitered, while the dews
    Fell fast I loitered still.

Song

Two doves upon the selfsame branch,
    Two lilies on a single stem,
Two butterflies upon one flower: —
    Oh happy they who look on them.

Who look upon them hand in hand
    Flushed in the rosy summer light;
Who look upon them hand in hand
    And never give a thought to night.

Maude Clare

Out of the church she followed them
  With a lofty step and mien:
His bride was like a village maid,
  Maude Clare was like a queen.

'Son Thomas,' his lady mother said,
  With smiles, almost with tears:
'May Nell and you but live as true
  As we have done for years;

'Your father thirty years ago
  Had just your tale to tell;
But he was not so pale as you,
  Nor I so pale as Nell.'

My lord was pale with inward strife,
  And Nell was pale with pride;
My lord gazed long on pale Maude Clare
  Or ever he kissed the bride.

'Lo, I have brought my gift, my lord,
  Have brought my gift,' she said:
'To bless the hearth, to bless the board,
  To bless the marriage-bed.

'Here's my half of the golden chain
  You wore about your neck,
That day we waded ankle-deep
  For lilies in the beck:

'Here's my half of the faded leaves
  We plucked from budding bough,
With feet amongst the lily leaves, —
  The lilies are budding now.'

He strove to match her scorn with scorn,
    He faltered in his place:
'Lady,' he said, — 'Maude Clare,' he said, —
    'Maude Clare:' — and hid his face.

She turn'd to Nell: 'My Lady Nell,
    I have a gift for you;
Though, were it fruit, the bloom were gone,
    Or, were it flowers, the dew.

'Take my share of a fickle heart,
    Mine of a paltry love:
Take it or leave it as you will,
    I wash my hands thereof.'

'And what you leave,' said Nell, 'I'll take,
    And what you spurn, I'll wear;
For he's my lord for better and worse,
    And him I love, Maude Clare.

'Yea, though you're taller by the head,
    More wise and much more fair;
I'll love him till he loves me best,
    Me best of all, Maude Clare.'

Echo

Come to me in the silence of the night;
    Come in the speaking silence of a dream:
Come with soft rounded cheeks and eyes as bright
    As sunlight on a stream;
    Come back in tears,
O memory, hope, love of finished years.

Oh dream how sweet, too sweet, too bitter sweet,
  Whose wakening should have been in Paradise,
Where souls brimfull of love abide and meet;
    Where thirsting longing eyes
      Watch the slow door
That opening, letting in, lets out no more.

Yet come to me in dreams, that I may live
  My very life again though cold in death:
Come back to me in dreams, that I may give
    Pulse for pulse, breath for breath:
      Speak low, lean low,
As long ago, my love, how long ago!

Another Spring

If I might see another Spring
  I'd not plant summer flowers and wait:
I'd have my crocuses at once,
My leafless pink mezereons,
    My chill-veined snowdrops, choicer yet
    My white or azure violet,
Leaf-nested primrose; anything
    To blow at once not late.

If I might see another Spring
  I'd listen to the daylight birds
That build their nests and pair and sing,
Nor wait for mateless nightingale;
    I'd listen to the lusty herds,
    The ewes with lambs as white as snow,
I'd find out music in the hail
    And all the winds that blow.

If I might see another Spring —
    Oh stinging comment on my past
That all my past results in 'if' —
    If I might see another Spring
I'd laugh to-day, to-day is brief;
I would not wait for anything:
    I'd use to-day that cannot last,
    Be glad to-day and sing.

May

I cannot tell you how it was;
But this I know: it came to pass
Upon a bright and breezy day
When May was young; ah, pleasant May!
As yet the poppies were not born
Between the blades of tender corn;
The last eggs had not hatched as yet,
Nor any bird forgone its mate.

    I cannot tell you what it was;
But this I know: it did but pass.
It passed away with sunny May,
With all sweet things it passed away,
And left me old, and cold, and grey.

A Pause of Thought

I looked for that which is not, nor can be,
    And hope deferred made my heart sick in truth:
But years must pass before a hope of youth
    Is resigned utterly.

I watched and waited with a steadfast will:
　　And though the object seemed to flee away
　　That I so longed for, ever day by day
　　　I watched and waited still.

Sometimes I said: This thing shall be no more;
　　My expectation wearies and shall cease;
　　I will resign it now and be at peace:
　　　Yet never gave it o'er.

Sometimes I said: It is an empty name
　　I long for; to a name why should I give
　　The peace of all the days I have to live? —
　　　Yet gave it all the same.

Alas, thou foolish one! alike unfit
　　For healthy joy and salutary pain:
　　Thou knowest the chase useless, and again
　　　Turnest to follow it.

Wife to Husband

Pardon the faults in me,
　　For the love of years ago
　　　Good-bye.
I must drift across the sea,
　　I must sink into the snow,
　　　I must die.

You can bask in this sun,
　　You can drink wine, and eat:
　　　Good-bye.
I must gird myself and run,
　　Though with unready feet:
　　　I must die.

Blank sea to sail upon,
  Cold bed to sleep in :
    Good-bye.
While you clasp, I must be gone
  For all your weeping :
    I must die.

A kiss for one friend,
  And a word for two, —
    Good-bye : —
A lock that you must send,
  A kindness you must do :
    I must die.

Not a word for you,
  Not a lock or kiss,
    Good-bye.
We, one, must part in two ;
  Verily death is this :
    I must die.

Song

When I am dead, my dearest,
  Sing no sad songs for me ;
Plant thou no roses at my head,
  Nor shady cypress tree :
Be the green grass above me
  With showers and dewdrops wet ;
And if thou wilt, remember,
  And if thou wilt, forget.
I shall not see the shadows,
  I shall not feel the rain ;
I shall not hear the nightingale
  Sing on, as if in pain :

And dreaming through the twilight
That doth not rise nor set,
Haply I may remember,
And haply may forget.

Bitter for Sweet

Summer is gone with all its roses,
Its sun and perfumes and sweet flowers,
Its warm air and refreshing showers:
And even Autumn closes.

Yea, Autumn's chilly self is going,
And winter comes which is yet colder;
Each day the hoar-frost waxes bolder
And the last buds cease blowing.

Sister Maude

Who told my mother of my shame,
Who told my father of my dear?
Oh who but Maude, my sister Maude,
Who lurked to spy and peer.

Cold he lies, as cold as stone,
With his clotted curls about his face:
The comeliest corpse in all the world
And worthy of a queen's embrace.

You might have spared his soul, sister,
Have spared my soul, your own soul too:
Though I had not been born at all,
He'd never have looked at you.

My father may sleep in Paradise,
    My mother at Heaven-gate:
But sister Maude shall get no sleep
    Either early or late.

My father may wear a golden gown,
    My mother a crown may win;
If my dear and I knocked at Heaven-gate
    Perhaps they'd let us in:
But sister Maude, oh sister Maude,
    Bide *you* with death and sin.

The First Spring Day

I wonder if the sap is stirring yet,
If wintry birds are dreaming of a mate,
If frozen snowdrops feel as yet the sun
And crocus fires are kindling one by one:
    Sing, robin, sing;
I still am sore in doubt concerning Spring.

I wonder if the springtide of this year
Will bring another Spring both lost and dear;
If heart and spirit will find out their Spring,
Or if the world alone will bud and sing:
    Sing, hope, to me;
Sweet notes, my hope, soft notes for memory.

The sap will surely quicken soon or late,
The tardiest bird will twitter to a mate;
So Spring must dawn again with warmth and bloom,
Or in this world, or in the world to come:
    Sing, voice of Spring,
Till I too blossom and rejoice and sing.

The Convent Threshold

There's blood between us, love, my love,
There's father's blood, there's brother's blood;
And blood's a bar I cannot pass:
I choose the stairs that mount above,
Stair after golden skyward stair,
To city and to sea of glass.
My lily feet are soiled with mud,
With scarlet mud which tells a tale
Of hope that was, of guilt that was,
Of love that shall not yet avail;
Alas, my heart, if I could bare
My heart, this selfsame stain is there:
I seek the sea of glass and fire
To wash the spot, to burn the snare;
Lo, stairs are meant to lift us higher:
Mount with me, mount the kindled stair.

Your eyes look earthward, mine look up.
I see the far-off city grand,
Beyond the hills a watered land,
Beyond the gulf a gleaming strand
Of mansions where the righteous sup;
Who sleep at ease among their trees,
Or wake to sing a cadenced hymn
With Cherubim and Seraphim;
They bore the Cross, they drained the cup,
Racked, roasted, crushed, wrenched limb from limb,
They the offscouring of the world:
The heaven of starry heavens unfurled,
The sun before their face is dim.

You looking earthward what see you?
Milk-white wine-flushed among the vines,
Up and down leaping, to and fro,
Most glad, most full, made strong with wines,

Blooming as peaches pearled with dew,
Their golden windy hair afloat,
Love-music warbling in their throat,
Young men and women come and go.

You linger, yet the time is short:
Flee for your life, gird up your strength
To flee; the shadows stretched at length
Show that day wanes, that night draws nigh;
Flee to the mountain, tarry not.
Is this a time for smile and sigh,
For songs among the secret trees
Where sudden blue birds nest and sport?
The time is short and yet you stay:
To-day while it is called to-day
Kneel, wrestle, knock, do violence, pray;
To-day is short, to-morrow nigh:
Why will you die? why will you die?

You sinned with me a pleasant sin:
Repent with me, for I repent.
Woe's me the lore I must unlearn!
Woe's me that easy way we went,
So rugged when I would return!
How long until my sleep begin,
How long shall stretch these nights and days?
Surely, clean Angels cry, she prays;
She laves her soul with tedious tears:
How long must stretch these years and years?

I turn from you my cheeks and eyes,
My hair which you shall see no more —
Alas for joy that went before,
For joy that dies, for love that dies.
Only my lips still turn to you,
My livid lips that cry, Repent.
Oh weary life, oh weary Lent,
Oh weary time whose stars are few.

How should I rest in Paradise,
Or sit on steps of heaven alone?
If Saints and Angels spoke of love
Should I not answer from my throne:
Have pity upon me, ye my friends,
For I have heard the sound thereof:
Should I not turn with yearning eyes,
Turn earthwards with a pitiful pang?
Oh save me from a pang in heaven.
By all the gifts we took and gave,
Repent, repent, and be forgiven:
This life is long, but yet it ends;
Repent and purge your soul and save:
No gladder song the morning stars
Upon their birthday morning sang
Than Angels sing when one repents.

I tell you what I dreamed last night:
A spirit with transfigured face
Fire-footed clomb an infinite space.
I heard his hundred pinions clang,
Heaven-bells rejoicing rang and rang,
Heaven-air was thrilled with subtle scents
Worlds spun upon their rushing cars:
He mounted shrieking: 'Give me light.'
Still light was poured on him, more light;
Angels, Archangels he outstripped
Exultant in exceeding might,
And trod the skirts of Cherubim.
Still 'Give me light,' he shrieked; and dipped
His thirsty face, and drank a sea,
Athirst with thirst it could not slake.
I saw him, drunk with knowledge, take
From aching brows the aureole crown —
His locks writhed like a cloven snake —
He left his throne to grovel down
And lick the dust of Seraph's feet:
For what is knowledge duly weighed?

Knowledge is strong but love is sweet;
Yea all the progress ye had made
Was but to learn that all is small
Save love, for love is all in all.

I tell you what I dreamed last night:
It was not dark, it was not light,
Cold dews had drenched my plenteous hair
Through clay; you came to seek me there.
And 'Do you dream of me?' you said.
My heart was dust that used to leap
To you; I answered half asleep:
'My pillow is damp, my sheets are red,
There's a leaden tester to my bed:
Find you a warmer playfellow,
A warmer pillow for your head,
A kinder love to love than mine.'
You wrung your hands; while I like lead
Crushed downwards through the sodden earth:
You smote your hands but not in mirth,
And reeled but were not drunk with wine.

For all night long I dreamed of you:
I woke and prayed against my will,
Then slept to dream of you again.
At length I rose and knelt and prayed:
I cannot write the words I said,
My words were slow, my tears were few;
But through the dark my silence spoke
Like thunder. When this morning broke,
My face was pinched, my hair was grey,
And frozen blood was on the sill
Where stifling in my struggle I lay.

If now you saw me you would say:
Where is the face I used to love?
And I would answer: Gone before;
It tarries veiled in paradise.

When once the morning star shall rise,
When earth with shadow flees away
And we stand safe within the door,
Then you shall lift the veil thereof.
Look up, rise up: for far above
Our palms are grown, our place is set;
There we shall meet as once we met
And love with old familiar love.

Up-Hill

Does the road wind up-hill all the way?
   Yes, to the very end.
Will the day's journey take the whole long day?
   From morn to night, my friend.

But is there for the night a resting-place?
   A roof for when the slow dark hours begin.
May not the darkness hide it from my face?
   You cannot miss that inn.

Shall I meet other wayfarers at night?
   Those who have gone before.
Then must I knock, or call when just in sight?
   They will not keep you standing at that door.

Shall I find comfort, travel-sore and weak?
   Of labour you shall find the sum.
Will there be beds for me and all who seek?
   Yea, beds for all who come.

'A Bruised Reed shall He not Break'

I will accept thy will to do and be,
  Thy hatred and intolerance of sin,
  Thy will at least to love, that burns within
    And thirsteth after Me:
So will I render fruitful, blessing still,
  The germs and small beginnings in thy heart,
  Because thy will cleaves to the better part. —
    Alas, I cannot will.

Dost not thou will, poor soul? Yet I receive
  The inner unseen longings of the soul,
  I guide them turning towards Me; I control
    And charm hearts till they grieve:
If thou desire, it yet shall come to pass,
  Though thou but wish indeed to choose My love;
  For I have power in earth and heaven above. —
    I cannot wish, alas!

What, neither choose nor wish to choose? and yet
  I still must strive to win thee and constrain:
  For thee I hung upon the cross in pain,
    How then can I forget?
If thou as yet dost neither love, nor hate,
  Nor choose, nor wish, — resign thyself, be still
  Till I infuse love, hatred, longing, will. —
    I do not deprecate.

A Better Resurrection

I have no wit, no words, no tears;
   My heart within me like a stone
Is numbed too much for hopes or fears;
   Look right, look left, I dwell alone;
I lift mine eyes, but dimmed with grief
   No everlasting hills I see;
My life is in the falling leaf:
     O Jesus, quicken me.

My life is like a faded leaf,
   My harvest dwindled to a husk;
Truly my life is void and brief
   And tedious in the barren dusk;
My life is like a frozen thing,
   No bud nor greenness can I see:
Yet rise it shall — the sap of Spring;
     O Jesus, rise in me.

My life is like a broken bowl,
   A broken bowl that cannot hold
One drop of water for my soul
   Or cordial in the searching cold;
Cast in the fire the perished thing,
   Melt and remould it, till it be
A royal cup for Him my King:
     O Jesus, drink of me.

The Three Enemies

THE FLESH

'Sweet, thou art pale.'
      'More pale to see,
Christ hung upon the cruel tree
And bore His Father's wrath for me.'

'Sweet, thou art sad.'
      'Beneath a rod
More heavy, Christ for my sake trod
The winepress of the wrath of God.'

'Sweet, thou art weary.'
      'Not so Christ:
Whose mighty love of me sufficed
For Strength, Salvation, Eucharist.'

'Sweet, thou art footsore.'
      'If I bleed,
His feet have bled: yea, in my need
His Heart once bled for mine indeed.'

THE WORLD

'Sweet, thou art young.'
      'So He was young
Who for my sake in silence hung
Upon the Cross with Passion wrung.'

'Look, thou art fair.'
      'He was more fair
Than men, Who deigned for me to wear
A visage marred beyond compare.'

'And thou hast riches.'
     'Daily bread:
All else is His; Who living, dead,
For me lacked where to lay His Head.'

'And life is sweet.'
     'It was not so
To Him, Whose cup did overflow
With mine unutterable woe.'

THE DEVIL

'Thou drinkest deep.'
     'When Christ would sup
He drained the dregs from out my cup:
So how should I be lifted up?'

'Thou shalt win Glory.'
     'In the skies,
Lord Jesus, cover up mine eyes
Lest they should look on vanities.'

'Thou shalt have Knowledge.'
     'Helpless dust!
In Thee, O Lord, I put my trust:
Answer Thou for me, Wise and Just.'

'And Might.' —
     'Get thee behind me. Lord,
Who hast redeemed and not abhorred
My soul, oh keep it by Thy Word.'

The One Certainty

Vanity of vanities, the Preacher saith,
  All things are vanity. The eye and ear
  Cannot be filled with what they see and hear.
Like early dew, or like the sudden breath
Of wind, or like the grass that withereth,
  Is man, tossed to and fro by hope and fear:
  So little joy hath he, so little cheer,
Till all things end in the long dust of death.
To-day is still the same as yesterday,
  To-morrow also even as one of them;
And there is nothing new under the sun:
Until the ancient race of Time be run,
  The old thorns shall grow out of the old stem,
And morning shall be cold and twilight grey.

Sweet Death

The sweetest blossoms die.
  And so it was that, going day by day
  Unto the Church to praise and pray,
And crossing the green churchyard thoughtfully,
  I saw how on the graves the flowers
  Shed their fresh leaves in showers,
And how their perfume rose up to the sky
  Before it passed away.

The youngest blossoms die.
  They die and fall and nourish the rich earth
  From which they lately had their birth;

Sweet life, but sweeter death that passeth by
   And is as though it had not been: —
   All colours turn to green;
The bright hues vanish and the odours fly,
   The grass hath lasting worth.

And youth and beauty die.
   So be it, O my God, Thou God of truth:
   Better than beauty and than youth
Are Saints and Angels, a glad company;
   And Thou, O Lord, our Rest and Ease,
   Art better far than these.
Why should be shrink from our full harvest? why
   Prefer to glean with Ruth?

Symbols

I watched a rosebud very long
   Brought on by dew and sun and shower,
   Waiting to see the perfect flower:
Then, when I thought it should be strong,
   It opened at the matin hour
And fell at evensong.

I watched a nest from day to day,
   A green nest full of pleasant shade,
   Wherein three speckled eggs were laid:
But when they should have hatched in May,
   The two old birds had grown afraid
Or tired, and flew away.

Then in my wrath I broke the bough
   That I had tended so with care,
   Hoping its scent should fill the air;
I crushed the eggs, not heeding how
   Their ancient promise had been fair:
I would have vengeance now.

But the dead branch spoke from the sod,
    And the eggs answered me again:
    Because we failed dost thou complain?
Is thy wrath just? And what if God,
    Who waiteth for thy fruits in vain,
Should also take the rod?

The World

SONNET

By day she woos me, soft, exceeding fair:
    But all night as the moon so changeth she;
    Loathsome and foul with hideous leprosy
And subtle serpents gliding in her hair.
By day she woos me to the outer air,
    Ripe fruit, sweet flowers, and full satiety:
    But through the night, a beast she grins at me,
A very monster void of love and prayer.
By day she stands a lie: by night she stands
    In all the naked horror of the truth
With pushing horns and clawed and clutching hands.
Is this a friend indeed; that I should sell
    My soul to her, give her my life and youth,
Till my feet, cloven too, take hold on hell?

Sleep at Sea

Sound the deep waters: —
    Who shall sound that deep? —
Too short the plummet,
    And the watchmen sleep.
Some dream of effort
    Up a toilsome steep;
Some dream of pasture grounds
    For harmless sheep.

White shapes flit to and fro
    From mast to mast;
They feel the distant tempest
    That nears them fast:
Great rocks are straight ahead,
    Great shoals not past;
They shout to one another
    Upon the blast.

Oh, soft the streams drop music
    Between the hills,
And musical the birds' nests
    Beside those rills:
The nests are types of home
    Love-hidden from ills,
The nests are types of spirits
    Love-music fills.

So dream the sleepers,
    Each man in his place;
The lightning shows the smile
    Upon each face:
The ship is driving, driving,
    It drives apace:
And sleepers smile, and spirits
    Bewail their case.

The lightning glares and reddens
    Across the skies;
It seems but sunset
    To those sleeping eyes.
When did the sun go down
    On such a wise?
From such a sunset
    When shall day arise?

'Wake,' call the spirits:
    But to heedless ears:
They have forgotten sorrows
    And hopes and fears;
They have forgotten perils
    And smiles and tears;
Their dream has held them long,
    Long years and years.

'Wake,' call the spirits again:
    But it would take
A louder summons
    To bid them awake.
Some dream of pleasure
    For another's sake;
Some dream, forgetful
    Of a lifelong ache.

One by one slowly,
    Ah, how sad and slow!
Wailing and praying
    The spirits rise and go:
Clear stainless spirits
    White as white as snow;
Pale spirits, wailing
    For an overthrow.

One by one flitting,
    Like a mournful bird
Whose song is tired at last
    For no mate heard.
The loving voice is silent,
    The useless word;
One by one flitting
    Sick with hope deferred.

Driving and driving,
  The ship drives amain:
While swift from mast to mast
  Shapes flat again,
Flit silent as the silence
  Where men lie slain;
Their shadow cast upon the sails
  Is like a stain.

No voice to call the sleepers,
  No hand to raise:
They sleep to death in dreaming,
  Of length of days.
Vanity of vanities,
  The Preacher says:
Vanity is the end
  Of all their ways.

Spring Quiet

Gone were but the Winter,
  Come were but the Spring,
I would go to a covert
  Where the birds sing;

Where in the whitethorn
  Singeth a thrush,
And a robin sings
  In the holly-bush.

Full of fresh scents
Are the budding boughs
Arching high over
  A cool green house:

Full of sweet scents,
    And whispering air
Which sayeth softly:
    'We spread no snare;

'Here dwell in safety,
    Here dwell alone,
With a clear stream
    And a mossy stone.

'Here the sun shineth
    Most shadily;
Here is heard an echo
    Of the far sea,
        Though far off it be.'

A Portrait

I

She gave up beauty in her tender youth,
    Gave up all hope and joy and pleasant ways;
    She covered up her eyes lest they should gaze
On vanity, and chose the bitter truth.
Harsh towards herself, towards others full of ruth,
    Servant of servants, little known to praise,
    Long prayers and fasts trenched on her nights and days:
She schooled herself to sights and sounds uncouth
That with the poor and stricken she might make
    A home, until the least of all sufficed
Her wants; her own self learned she to forsake,
Counting all earthly gain but hurt and loss.
So with calm will she chose and bore the cross
    And hated all for love of Jesus Christ.

II

They knelt in silent anguish by her bed,
  And could not weep; but calmly there she lay.
  All pain had left her; and the sun's last ray
Shone through upon her, warming into red
The shady curtains. In her heart she said:
  'Heaven opens; I leave these and go away;
  The Bridegroom calls, — shall the Bride seek to stay?'
Then low upon her breast she bowed her head.
O lily flower, O gem of priceless worth,
  O dove with patient voice and patient eyes,
O fruitful vine amid a land of dearth,
  O maid replete with loving purities,
Thou bowedst down thy head with friends on earth
  To raise it with the saints in Paradise.

Dream-Love

Young Love lies sleeping
  In May-time of the year,
Among the lilies,
  Lapped in the tender light:
White lambs come grazing,
  White doves come building there;
And round about him
  The May-bushes are white.

Soft moss the pillow
  For oh, a softer cheek;
Broad leaves cast shadow
  Upon the heavy eyes:
There winds and waters
  Grow lulled and scarcely speak;
There twilight lingers
  The longest in the skies.

Young Love lies dreaming;
  But who shall tell the dream?
A perfect sunlight
  On rustling forest tips;
Or perfect moonlight
  Upon a rippling stream;
Or perfect silence,
  Or song of cherished lips.

Burn odours round him
  To fill the drowsy air;
Weave silent dances
  Around him to and fro;
For oh, in waking
  The sights are not so fair,
And song and silence
  Are not like these below.

Young Love lies dreaming
  Till summer days are gone, —
Dreaming and drowsing
  Away to perfect sleep:
He sees the beauty
  Sun hath not looked upon,
And tastes the fountain
  Unutterably deep.

Him perfect music
  Doth hush unto his rest,
And through the pauses
  The perfect silence calms:
Oh, poor the voices
  Of earth from east to west,
And poor earth's stillness
  Between her stately palms.

Young Love lies drowsing
    Away to poppied death;
Cool shadows deepen
    Across the sleeping face:
So fails the summer
    With warm, delicious breath;
And what hath autumn
    To give us in its place?

Draw close the curtains
    Of branched evergreen;
Change cannot touch them
    With fading fingers sere:
Here the first violets
    Perhaps will bud unseen,
And a dove, may be,
    Return to nestle here.

Twice

I took my heart in my hand
    (O my love, O my love),
I said: Let me fall or stand,
    Let me live or die,
But this once hear me speak —
    (O my love, O my love) —
Yet a woman's words are weak;
    You should speak, not I.

You took my heart in your hand
    With a friendly smile,
With a critical eye you scanned,
    Then set it down,
And said: It is still unripe,
    Better wait awhile;
Wait while the skylarks pipe,
    Till the corn grows brown.

As you set it down it broke —
  Broke, but I did not wince;
I smiled at the speech you spoke,
  At your judgment that I heard:
But I have not often smiled
  Since then, nor questioned since,
Nor cared for corn-flowers wild,
  Nor sung with the singing bird.

I take my heart in my hand,
  O my God, O my God,
My broken heart in my hand:
  Thou hast seen, judge Thou.
My hope was written on sand,
  O my God, O my God:
Now let Thy judgment stand —
  Yea, judge me now.

This contemned of a man,
  This marred one heedless day,
This heart take Thou to scan
  Both within and without:
Refine with fire its gold,
  Purge Thou its dross away —
Yea, hold it in Thy hold,
  Whence none can pluck it out.

I take my heart in my hand —
  I shall not die, but live —
Before Thy face I stand;
  I, for Thou callest such:
All that I have I have I bring,
  All that I am I give,
Smile Thou and I shall sing,
  But shall not question much.

One Day

I will tell you when they met:
In the limpid days of Spring;
Elder boughs were budding yet,
Oaken boughs looked wintry still,
But primrose and veined violet
In the mossful turf were set,
While meeting birds made haste to sing
And build with right good will.

I will tell you when they parted:
When plenteous Autumn sheaves were brown,
Then they parted heavy-hearted;
The full rejoicing sun looked down
As grand as in the days before;
Only they had lost a crown;
Only to them those days of yore
Could come back nevermore.

When shall they meet? I cannot tell,
Indeed, when they shall meet again,
Except some day in Paradise:
For this they wait, one waits in pain.
Beyond the sea of death love lies
For ever, yesterday, to-day;
Angels shall ask them, 'Is it well?'
And they shall answer, 'Yea.'

A Dream

Once in a dream (for once I dreamed of you)
    We stood together in an open field;
    Above our heads two swift-winged pigeons wheeled,
Sporting at ease and courting full in view.
When loftier still a broadening darkness flew,
    Down-swooping, and a ravenous hawk revealed;
    Too weak to fight, too fond to fly, they yield;
So farewell life and love and pleasures new.
Then as their plumes fell fluttering to the ground,
    Their snow-white plumage flecked with crimson drops,
    I wept, and thought I turned towards you to weep:
But you were gone; while rustling hedgerow tops
Bent in a wind which bore to me a sound
    Of far-off piteous bleat of lambs and sheep.

Beauty is Vain

While roses are so red,
    While lilies are so white,
Shall a woman exalt her face
    Because it gives delight?
She's not so sweet as a rose,
    A lily's straighter than she,
And if she were as red or white
    She'd be but one of three.

Whether she flush in love's summer
    Or in its winter grow pale,
Whether she flaunt her beauty
    Or hide it away in a veil,

72

Be she red or white,
   And stand she erect or bowed,
Time will win the race he runs with her
   And hide her away in a shroud.

What would I Give?

What would I give for a heart of flesh to warm me
   through,
Instead of this heart of stone ice-cold whatever I do;
Hard and cold and small, of all hearts the worst of all.

What would I give for words, if only words would come;
But now in its misery my spirit has fallen dumb:
Oh, merry friends, go your way, I have never a word to say.

What would I give for tears, not smiles but scalding tears,
To wash the black mark clean, and to thaw the frost of
   years,
To wash the stain ingrain and to make me clean again.

The Bourne

Underneath the growing grass,
   Underneath the living flowers,
   Deeper than the sound of showers:
   There we shall not count the hours
By the shadows as they pass.

Youth and health will be but vain,
    Beauty reckoned of no worth:
    There a very little girth
    Can hold round what once the earth
Seemed too narrow to contain.

Memory

I

I nursed it in my bosom while it lived,
    I hid it in my heart when it was dead;
In joy I sat alone, even so I grieved
    Alone and nothing said.

I shut the door to face the naked truth,
    I stood alone — I faced the truth alone,
Stripped bare of self-regard or forms or ruth
    Till first and last were shown.

I took the perfect balances and weighed;
    No shaking of my hand disturbed the poise;
Weighed, found it wanting: not a word I said,
    But silent made my choice.

None know the choice I made; I make it still.
    None know the choice I made and broke my heart,
Breaking mine idol: I have braced my will
    Once, chosen for once my part.

I broke it at a blow, I laid it cold,
    Crushed in my deep heart where it used to live.
My heart dies inch by inch; the time grows old,
    Grows old in which I grieve.

I have a room whereinto no one enters
    Save I myself alone:
    There sits a blessed memory on a throne,
There my life centres.

While winter comes and goes — oh tedious comer! —
    And while its nip-wind blows;
    While bloom the bloodless lily and warm rose
Of lavish summer.

If any should force entrance he might see there
    One buried yet not dead,
    Before whose face I no more bow my head
Or bend my knee there;

But often in my worn life's autumn weather
    I watch there with clear eyes,
    And think how it will be in Paradise
When we're together.

Shall I forget?

Shall I forget on this side of the grave?
I promise nothing: you must wait and see
    Patient and brave.
(O my soul, watch with him and he with me.)

Shall I forget in peace of Paradise?
I promise nothing: follow, friend, and see
    Faithful and wise.
(O my soul, lead the way he walks with me.)

Vanity of Vanities

Ah, woe is me for pleasure that is vain,
  Ah, woe is me for glory that is past:
  Pleasure that bringeth sorrow at the last,
Glory that at the last bringeth no gain!
So saith the sinking heart; and so again
  It shall say till the mighty angel-blast
  Is blown, making the sun and moon aghast
And showering down the stars like sudden rain.
And evermore men shall go fearfully
  Bending beneath their weight of heaviness;
And ancient men shall lie down wearily,
  And strong men shall rise up in weariness;
Yea, even the young shall answer sighingly
  Saying one to another: How vain it is!

L.E.L.

'Whose heart was breaking for a little love.'

Downstairs I laugh, I sport and jest with all:
  But in my solitary room above
I turn my face in silence to the wall;
  My heart is breaking for a little love.
    Though winter frosts are done,
    And birds pair every one,
And leaves peep out, for springtide is begun.

I feel no spring, while spring is wellnigh blown,
  I find no nest, while nests are in the grove:
Woe's me for mine own heart that dwells alone,

76

My heart that breakethf or a little love.
    While golden in the sun
    Rivulets rise and run,
While lilies bud, for springtide is begun.

All love, are loved, save only I ; their hearts
   Beat warm with love and joy, beat full thereof :
They cannot guess, who play the pleasant parts,
   My heart is breaking for a little love.
    While beehives wake and whirr,
    And rabbit thins his fur,
In living spring that sets the world astir.

I deck myself with silks and jewelry,
   I plume myself like any mated dove :
They praise my rustling show, and never see
   My heart is breaking for a little love.
    While sprouts green lavender
    With rosemary and myrrh,
For in quick spring the sap is all astir.

Perhaps some saints in glory guess the truth,
   Perhaps some angels read it as they move,
And cry one to another full of ruth,
   'Her heart is breaking for a little love.'
    Though other things have birth,
    And leap and sing for mirth,
When springtime wakes and clothes and feeds the earth.

Yet saith a saint : 'Take patience for thy scathe ;'
   Yet saith an angel : 'Wait, for thou shalt prove
True best is last, true life is born of death,
   O thou, heart-broken for a little love.
    Then love shall fill thy girth,
    And love make fat thy dearth,
When new spring builds new heaven and clean new
   earth.'

Life and Death

Life is not sweet. One day it will be sweet
    To shut our eyes and die:
Nor feel the wild flowers blow, nor birds dart by
    With flitting butterfly,
Nor grass grow long above our heads and feet,
Nor hear the happy lark that soars sky high,
Nor sigh that spring is fleet and summer fleet,
    Nor mark the waxing wheat,
Nor know who sits in our accustomed seat.

Life is not good. One day it will be good
    To die, then live again;
To sleep meanwhile: so not to feel the wane
Of shrunk leaves dropping in the wood,
Nor hear the foamy lashing of the main,
Nor mark the blackened bean-fields, nor where stood
    Rich ranks of golden grain
Only dead refuse stubble clothe the plain:
Asleep from risk, asleep from pain.

Grown and Flown

I loved my love from green of Spring
    Until sere Autumn's fall;
But now that leaves are withering
    How should one love at all?
    One heart's too small
For hunger, cold , love, everything.

I loved my love on sunny days
    Until late Summer's wane;

But now that frost begins to glaze
 How should one love again?
 Nay, love and pain
Walk wide apart in diverse ways.

I loved my love — alas to see
 That this should be, alas!
I thought that this could scarcely be,
 Yet has it come to pass:
 Sweet sweet love was,
Now bitter bitter grown to me.

Somewhere or Other

Somewhere or other there must surely be
 The face not seen, the voice not heard,
The heart that not yet — never yet — ah me!
 Made answer to my word.

Somewhere or other, may be near or far;
 Past land and sea, clean out of sight;
Beyond the wandering moon, beyond the star
 That tracks her night by night.

Somewhere or other, may be far or near;
 With just a wall, a hedge, between;
With just the last leaves of the dying year
 Fallen on a turf grown green.

Gone for Ever

O happy rose-bud blooming
  Upon thy parent tree,
Nay, thou art too presuming;
For soon the earth entombing
  Thy faded charms shall be,
And the chill damp consuming.

O happy skylark springing
  Up to the broad blue sky,
Too fearless in thy winging,
Too gladsome in thy singing,
  Thou also soon shalt lie
Where no sweet notes are ringing.

And through life's shine and shower
  We shall have joy and pain;
But in the summer bower,
And at the morning hour,
  We shall still look in vain
For the same bird and flower.

Despised and Rejected

My sun has set, I dwell
In darkness as a dead man out of sight;
And none remains, not one, that I should tell
To him mine evil plight
This bitter night.
I will make fast my door
That hollow friends may trouble me no more.

'Friend, open to Me.' — Who is this that calls?
Nay, I am deaf as are my walls:
Cease crying, for I will not hear
Thy cry of hope or fear.
Others were dear,
Others forsook me: what art thou indeed
That I should heed
Thy lamentable need?
Hungry should feed,
Or stranger lodge thee here?

'Friend, My Feet bleed.
Open thy door to Me and comfort Me.'
I will not open, trouble me no more.
Go on thy way footsore,
I will not rise and open unto thee.
'Then is it nothing to thee? Open, see
Who stands to plead with thee.
Open, lest I should pass thee by, and thou
One day entreat My Face
And howl for grace,
And I be deaf as thou art now.
Open to Me.'

Then I cried out upon him: Cease,
Leave me in peace:
Fear not that I should crave
Aught thou mayst have.
Leave me in peace, yea trouble me no more,
Lest I arise and chase thee from my door.
What, shall I not be let
Alone, that thou dost vex me yet?

But all night long that voice spake urgently:
'Open to Me.'
Still harping in mine ears:
'Rise, let Me in.'
Pleading with tears:
'Open to Me that I may come to thee.'

While the dew dropped, while the dark hours were cold:
'My Feet bleed, see My Face,
See My Hands bleed that bring thee grace,
My Heart doth bleed for thee,
Open to Me.'

So till the break of day:
Then died away
That voice, in silence as of sorrow;
Then footsteps echoing like a sigh
Passed me by,
Lingering footsteps slow to pass.
On the morrow
I saw upon the grass
Each footprint marked in blood, and on my door
The mark of blood for evermore.

Long Barren

Thou who didst hang upon a barren tree,
My God, for me;
   Though I till now be barren, now at length,
   Lord, give me strength
To bring forth fruit to Thee.

Thou who didst bear for me the crown of thorn,
Spitting and scorn;
   Though I till now have put forth thorns, yet now
   Strengthen me Thou
That better fruit be borne.

Thou Rose of Sharon, Cedar of broad roots,
Vine of sweet fruits,
   Thou Lily of the vale with fadeless leaf,
   Of thousands Chief,
Feed Thou my feeble shoots.

If Only

If I might only love my God and die!
　　But now He bids me love Him and live on,
　　Now when the bloom of all my life is gone,
The pleasant half of life has quite gone by.
My tree of hope is lopped that spread so high;
　　And I forget how summer glowed and shone,
　　While autumn grips me with its fingers wan,
　　And frets me with its fitful windy sigh.
When autumn passes then must winter numb,
　　And winter may not pass a weary while,
　　　But when it passes spring shall flower again:
And in that spring who weepeth now shall smile,
　　Yes, they shall wax who now are on the wane,
Yea, they shall sing for love when Christ shall come.

Dost Thou note Care?

I love and love not: Lord, it breaks my heart
　　To love and not to love.
Thou veiled within Thy glory, gone apart
　　Into Thy shrine, which is above,
Dost thou not love me, Lord, or care
　　For this mine ill? —
I love thee here or there,
　　I will accept thy broken heart, lie still.

Lord, it was well with me in time gone by
　　That cometh not again,
When I was fresh and cheerful, who but I?
　　I fresh, I cheerful: worn with pain

Now, out of sight and out of heart;
    O Lord, how long? —
I watch thee as thou art,
    I will accept thy fainting heart, be strong.

'Lie still,' 'be strong,' to-day; but, Lord, to-morrow,
    What of to-morrow, Lord?
Shall there be rest from toil, be truce from sorrow,
    Be living green upon the sward
Now but a barren grave to me,
    Be joy for sorrow? —
Did I not die for thee?
    Do I not live for thee? leave Me to-morrow.

Weary in Well-doing

I would have gone; God bade me stay:
    I would have worked; God bade me rest.
He broke my will from day to day,
    He read my yearnings unexpressed
        And said them nay.

Now I would stay; God bids me go:
    Now I would rest; God bids me work.
He breaks my heart tossed to and fro,
    My soul is wrung with doubts that lurk
        And vex it so.

I go, Lord, where Thou sendest me;
    Day after day I plod and moil:
But, Christ my God, when will it be
    That I may let alone my toil
        And rest with Thee?

Good Friday

Am I a stone and not a sheep
    That I can stand, O Christ, beneath Thy Cross,
    To number drop by drop Thy Blood's slow loss,
And yet not weep?

Not so those women loved
    Who with exceeding grief lamented Thee;
    Not so fallen Peter weeping bitterly;
Not so the thief was moved;

Not so the Sun and Moon
    Which hid their faces in a starless sky,
    A horror of great darkness at broad noon —
I, only I.

Yet give not o'er,
    But seek Thy sheep, true Shepherd of the flock;
    Greater than Moses, turn and look once more
And smite a rock.

The Lowest Place

Give me the lowest place: not that I dare
    Ask for that lowest place, but Thou hast died
That I might live and share
    Thy glory by Thy side.

Give me the lowest place: or if for me
    That lowest place too high, make one more low
Where I may sit and see
    My God and love Thee so.

Death's Chill Between

(*Athenaeum*, October 14, 1848)

Chide not; let me breathe a little,
   For I shall not mourn him long;
Though the life-cord was so brittle,
   The love-cord was very strong.
I would wake a little space
Till I find a sleeping-place.

You can go, — I shall not weep;
   You can go unto your rest.
My heart-ache is all too deep,
   And too sore my throbbing breast.
Can sobs be, or angry tears,
Where are neither hopes nor fears?

Though with you I am alone
   And must be so everywhere,
I will make no useless moan, —
   None shall say 'She could not bear:'
While life lasts I will be strong, —
But I shall not struggle long.

Listen, listen! Everywhere
   A low voice is calling me,
And a step is on the stair,
   And one comes ye do not see,
Listen, listen! Evermore
A dim hand knocks at the door.

Hear me; he is come again,—
   My own dearest is come back.
Bring him in from the cold rain;
   Bring wine, and let nothing lack.

Thou and I will rest together,
Love, until the sunny weather.

I will shelter thee from harm, —
    Hide thee from all heaviness.
Come to me, and keep thee warm
    By my side in quietness.
I will lull thee to thy sleep
With sweet songs : — we will not weep.

Who hath talked of weeping? — Yet
    There is something at my heart,
Gnawing, I would fain forget,
    And an aching and a smart.
— Ah ! my mother, 'tis in vain,
For he is *not* come again.

Heart's Chill Between

(*Athenaeum*, October 21, 1848)

I did not chide him, though I knew
    That he was false to me.
Chide the exhaling of the dew,
    The ebbing of the sea,
The fading of a rosy hue, —
    But not inconstancy.

Why strive for love when love is o'er?
    Why bind a restive heart? —
He never knew the pain I bore
    In saying : 'We must part ;
Let us be friends and nothing more.'
    — Oh, woman's shallow art !

But it is over, it is done, —
  I hardly heed it now;
So many weary years have run
  Since then, I think not how
Things might have been, — but greet each one
  With an unruffled brow.

What time I am where others be,
  My heart seems very calm —
Stone calm; but if all go from me,
  There comes a vague alarm,
A shrinking in the memory
  From some forgotten harm.

And often through the long, long night,
  Waking when none are near,
I feel my heart beat fast with fright,
  Yet know not what I fear.
Oh how I long to see the light,
  And the sweet birds to hear!

To have the sun upon my face,
  To look up through the trees,
To walk forth in the open space
  And listen to the breeze, —
And not to dream the burial-place
  Is clogging my weak knees.

Sometimes I can nor weep nor pray,
  But am half stupefied:
And then all those who see me say
  Mine eyes are opened wide
And that my wits seem gone away —
  Ah, would that I had died!

Would I could die and be at peace,
  Or living could forget

My grief nor grows nor doth decrease,
    But ever is : — and yet
Methinks, now, that all this shall cease
    Before the sun shall set.

Consider

(*Macmillan's Magazine*, Jan. 1866)

Consider
The lilies of the field whose bloom is brief : —
    We are as they ;
    Like them we fade away,
As doth a leaf.

Consider
The sparrows of the air of small account :
    Our God doth view
Whether they fall or mount, —
    He guards us too.

Consider
The lilies that do neither spin nor toil,
    Yet are most fair : —
    What profits all this care
And all this coil?

Consider
The birds that have no barn nor harvest-weeks ;
    God gives them food : —
Much more our Father seeks
    To do us good.

A Smile and a Sigh

(*Macmillan's Magazine*, May 1868)

A smile because the nights are short!
  And every morning brings such pleasure
Of sweet love-making, harmless sport:
  Love, that makes and finds its treasure;
  Love, treasure without measure.

A sigh because the days are long!
  Long long these days that pass in sighing,
A burden saddens every song:
  While time lags who should be flying,
  We live who would be dying.

'They Desire a Better Country'

(*Macmillan's Magazine*, March 1869)

I

I would not if I could undo my past,
  Tho' for its sake my future is a blank;
  My past, for which I have myself to thank
For all its faults and follies first and last.
I would not cast anew the lot once cast,
  Or launch a second ship for one that sank,
  Or drug with sweets the bitterness I drank,
Or break by feasting my perpetual fast.
I would not if I could: for much more dear
  Is one remembrance than a hundred joys,
    More than a thousand hopes in jubilee;
  Dearer the music of one tearful voice
    That unforgotten calls and calls to me,
'Follow me here, rise up, and follow here.'

II

What seekest thou far in the unknown land?
  In hope I follow joy gone on before,
  In hope and fear persistent more and more,
As the dry desert lengthens out its sand.
Whilst day and night I carry in my hand
  The golden key to ope the golden door
  Of golden home; yet mine eye weepeth sore
For the long journey that must make no stand.
And who is this that veiled doth walk with thee?
  Lo, this is Love that walketh at my right;
    One exile holds us both, and we are bound
To selfsame home-joys in the land of light.
Weeping thou walkest with him; weepeth he? —
    Some sobbing weep, some weep and make no sound.

III

A dimness of a glory glimmers here
  Thro' veils and distance from the space remote,
  A faintest far vibration of a note
Reaches to us and seems to bring us near,
Causing our face to glow with braver cheer,
  Making the serried mist to stand afloat,
  Subduing languor with an antidote,
And strengthening love almost to cast out fear,
Till for one moment golden city walls
  Rise looming on us, golden walls of home,
Light of our eyes until the darkness falls;
  Then thro' the outer darkness burdensome
I hear again the tender voice that calls,
  'Follow me hither, follow, rise, and come.'

Paradise: In a Dream

(*Lyra Messianica*, second edition, 1865)

Once in a dream I saw the flowers
   That bud and bloom in Paradise;
   More fair they are than waking eyes
Have seen in all this world of ours.
And faint the perfume-bearing rose,
   And faint the lily on its stem,
And faint the perfect violet
    Compared with them.

I heard the songs of Paradise:
   Each bird sat singing in his place;
   A tender song so full of grace
It soared like incense to the skies.
Each bird sat singing to his mate
   Soft cooing notes among the trees:
The nightingale herself were cold
    To such as these.

I saw the fourfold River flow,
   And deep it was, with golden sand;
   It flowed between a mossy land
Which murmured music grave and low.
It hath refreshment for all thirst,
   For fainting spirits strength and rest:
Earth holds not such a draught as this
    From east to west.

The Tree of Life stood budding there,
   Abundant with its twelvefold fruits;
   Eternal sap sustains its roots,
Its shadowing branches fill the air.

Its leaves are healing for the world,
   Its fruit the hungry world can feed,
Sweeter than honey to the taste
      And balm indeed.

I saw the gate called Beautiful;
   And looked, but scarce could look, within;
   I saw the golden streets begin,
And outskirts of the glassy pool.
Oh harps, oh crowns of plenteous stars,
   Oh green palm-branches many-leaved —
Eye hath not seen, nor ear hath heard,
      Nor heart conceived.

I hope to see these things again,
   But not as once in dreams by night;
   To see them with my very sight,
And touch, and handle, and attain:
To have all Heaven beneath my feet
   For narrow way that once they trod;
To have my part with all the Saints,
      And with my God.

Index of First Lines